A-Z of Snakes

A-Z of Snakes

Tom Jackson

amber
BOOKS

Published by
Amber Books Ltd
United House
North Road
London
N7 9DP
United Kingdom
www.amberbooks.co.uk
Appstore: itunes.com/apps/amberbooksltd
Facebook: www.facebook.com/amberbooks
Twitter: @amberbooks

ISBN: 978-1-78274-566-2

Project Editor: Sarah Uttridge
Design: Keren Harragan

All artworks © IMP AB apart from p22, 29 and 31 (© Amber Books Ltd)
Additional artworks by JB Illustrations

Printed in China

Contents

Anaconda

World's biggest snake.

Anacondas grow to 8 metres (26 feet) and weigh three times more than a man.

This snake lives in the rivers and swamps of South America.

Skeleton

It has almost 400 bones in its spine. Humans have just 33.

Coil Grip

It crushes its prey (other animals that it eats) by coiling its long body around it.

Boa Constrictor

Rainforest hunter.

Bite Defense
A Boa Constrictor bites attackers but does not use venom (poison) to kill prey.

Prey
It kills prey by squeezing it to death.

Young Boa Constrictors hunt in trees but older, heavier ones stay on the ground.

7

Cc

Coral Snake

Bright but deadly.

This snake lives in shallow swamps or slithers through mud and fallen leaves.

Food
It kills frogs, lizards and birds with a poisonous bite.

Colour Pattern
The red, yellow and then black pattern is a warning to stay away.

8

Death Adder

Lives in Australian forests.

The adder's venom can kill a human in less than six hours.

Ambush

This snake hides in leaves and twigs and pounces when prey comes past.

Stripes

The stripes make it hard to spot among leaves.

The Death Adder twitches its tail to attract prey.

9

Ee

European Adder

Most widespread snake.

The adder lives in more places than any other snake. It is found from Britain to Korea.

Bite
Adders use venom but their bites are not dangerous to people.

Winter Sleep
Adders stay underground during the cold winter.

Fer-de-Lance

Ff

From South America.

Babies
Mothers give birth to 70 baby snakes at a time.

Head
The snake has a triangle-shaped head like an arrowhead.

Its name means 'spearhead' in French.

Gg Green Tree Python

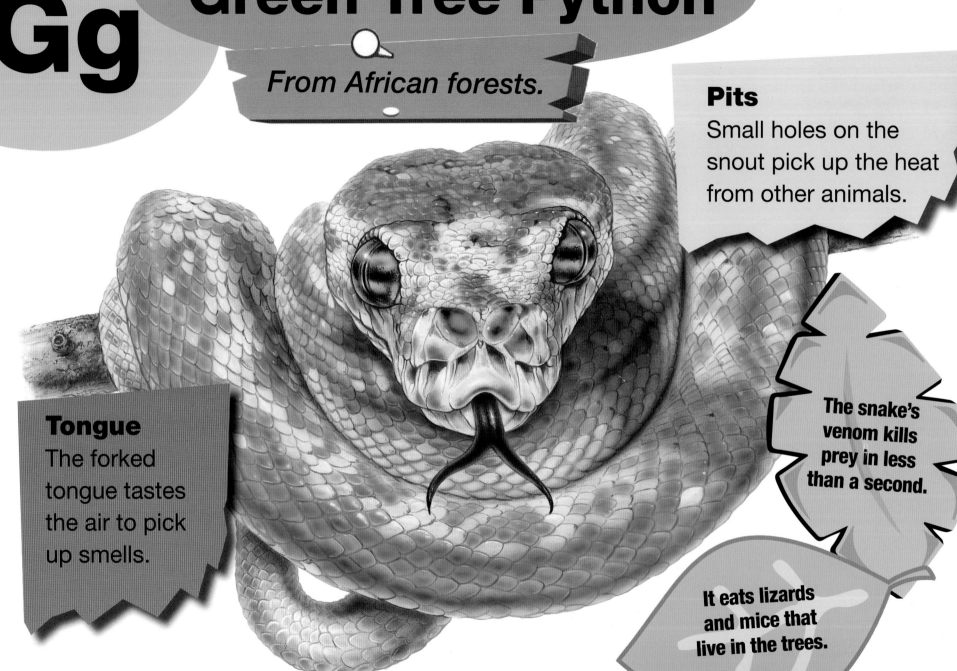

From African forests.

Pits
Small holes on the snout pick up the heat from other animals.

Tongue
The forked tongue tastes the air to pick up smells.

The snake's venom kills prey in less than a second.

It eats lizards and mice that live in the trees.

12

Horned Palm Viper

From Central America.

Eyes

Its eyes open wide in the dark. It can see colour, but not much detail.

Eyelashes

The horns above the eye help the snake hide in leaves.

The mother gives birth to 12 or more young. Each of these can be a different colour.

13

Ii

Inland Taipan

Most poisonous snake.

Fierce
This Australian reptile is also known as the fierce snake.

Deadly Bite
The venom in one bite from this snake is enough to kill 100 people in one hour!

The Inland Taipan lives in the desert. It is shy and stays away from people.

Jumping Viper

From Central America.

Big Mouth

This snake opens its mouth very wide to scare away large attackers.

This bulky snake lives in the rainforest.

Attack

This viper can lunge forward to bite prey very fast and may take off into the air.

15

Kk

King Cobra

From Indian rainforest.

Warning
This snake opens its hood to warn away attackers.

The King Cobra eats other snakes, even other cobras.

Big Biter
At 4 metres (13 feet) the King Cobra is the longest venomous snake in the world.

Long-Nosed Tree Snake

From Southeast Asia.

Thin Body
This slender reptile is also called a vine snake.

Take Aim
The grooves in the snout work like a gunsight so the snake can target its prey before striking.

This snake grabs frogs and other prey with its big mouth.

17

Mm

Massasauga

North American rattler.

Dark Skin
The baby snakes are pale with dark markings. The skin gets darker as they grow older.

Swamp
This small rattlesnake lives in marshes and swampy places.

'Massasauga' means 'river mouth'. The snakes often live near wide rivers.

North African Horned Viper

Nn

Hiding Out

This snake waits for prey buried under the sand with just its eyes showing.

Scales

To scare off enemies, it makes a loud noise by rubbing its scales together.

It hunts at night when the small animals that it eats come out.

Oo

Ornate Flying Snake

Lives in southeast Asian forests.

Jumps
It can jump from tree to tree when hunting, or glide to the ground.

Eyes
It has large eyes and good vision for hunting in daylight.

The female lays eggs in a tree.

Puff Adder

Lives in African grasslands.

Pp

The tough fangs can bite through thick clothing.

Loud Hiss
When frightened by an attacker, this snake puffs up its body and makes a loud hiss.

It hunts at night and kills birds, mice and lizards.

Up and Down
The Puff Adder can swim well and climb into trees and bushes.

Qq

Queen Snake

American river snake.

Fussy Eater
It eats mostly crayfish; little lobsters that live in rivers.

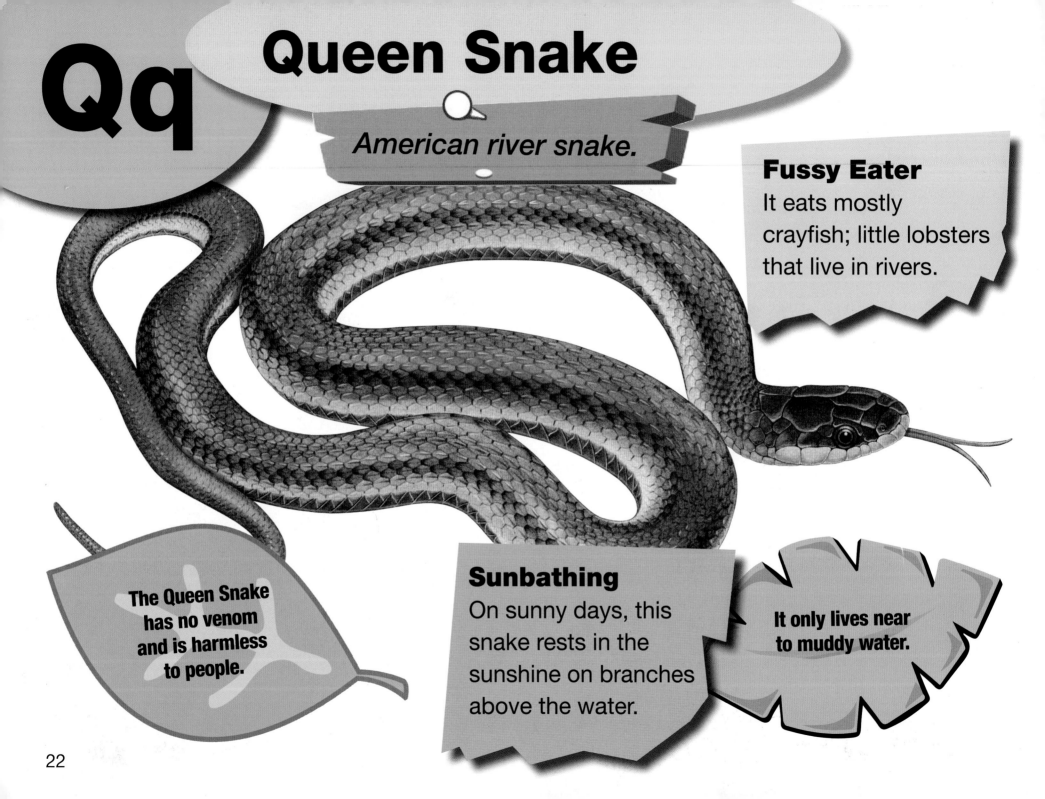

The Queen Snake has no venom and is harmless to people.

Sunbathing
On sunny days, this snake rests in the sunshine on branches above the water.

It only lives near to muddy water.

Rattlesnake

Found in American deserts.

Dead Skin

Beads of hard skin on the tail make a frightening rattle noise.

Markings

It is sometimes called a diamondback because of the brown shapes along its body.

The rattle gets longer, adding new beads, as the snake gets older.

23

Ss

Saw-Scaled Viper

Lives in dry parts of South Asia.

It is only 60 centimetres (24 inches) long.

Deadly
This snake is very dangerous. Its bites kill hundreds of people each year.

Mixed Food
This little snake eats mice, lizards, scorpions and insects.

During the day, the snake hides under rocks.

Tiger Snake

Found in wetland areas of Australia.

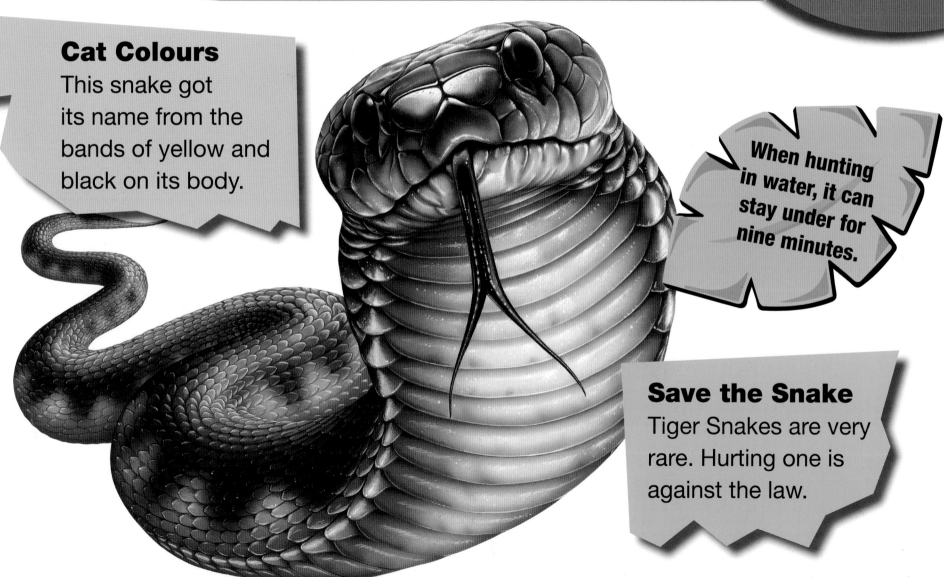

Cat Colours
This snake got its name from the bands of yellow and black on its body.

When hunting in water, it can stay under for nine minutes.

Save the Snake
Tiger Snakes are very rare. Hurting one is against the law.

Unusual Snakes

The weird and wonderful.

Worm Snake

The world's smallest snake lives in Barbados. It is only 10 cm (4 inches) long.

Rinkhals (right)

Grass snakes, like this one, lie still with the tongue out to fool attackers that they are dead.

Snakes always swallow prey head first.

Variable Bush Viper

From Central Africa.

Spiky Body
This snake's scales have a ridge in them which makes the skin very rough.

It can be varied colours: green, blue, brown, yellow and grey.

Jungle
It lives in rainforests and climbs in the short bushes close to the ground.

27

Ww Western Green Mamba

Lives in west African forests.

Powerful Bite
It gives a loud hiss when cornered and will bite over and over.

This slender snake climbs through trees, and goes higher to escape attackers.

Tree Food
It mainly eats birds and a few squirrels.

28

Xenopeltidae

Xx

Also called a Sunbeam Snake.

Rainbow
This snake has shiny skin which glimmers with many colours in the light.

Underground
It spends the day in burrows and hunts at night for frogs.

It lives in Southeast Asia.

Yy

Yellow-Bellied Sea Snake

Lives in oceans.

Swimmer
The tail is flattened into a paddle to help with swimming.

This snake is not strong enough to slither on land.

Water Snake
This sea snake never comes on land. It gives birth to babies on floating seaweeds.

It breathes air, drinks rain and eats fish.

Zebra Spitting Cobra

From southern Africa.

Spray
This snake can squirt its venom at attackers, such as eagles.

It has black and white stripes like a zebra.

It can lift the first third of its body into the air.

In the Nest
It lays about 15 eggs and protects them until they hatch.

31

Aa
Anaconda

Bb
Boa Constrictor

Cc
Coral Snake

Dd
Death Adder

Ee
European Adder

Ff
Fer-de-Lance

Gg
Green Tree Python

Hh
Horned Palm Viper

Ii
Inland Taipan

Jj
Jumping Viper

Kk
King Cobra

Ll
Long-Nosed Tree Snake

Mm
Massasauga

Nn
North African Horned Viper

Oo
Ornate Flying Snake

Pp
Puff Adder

Qq
Queen Snake

Rr
Rattlesnake

Ss
Saw-Scaled Viper

Tt
Tiger Snake

Uu
Unusual Snakes

Vv
Variable Bush Viper

Ww
Western Green Mamba

Xx
Xenopeltidae

Yy
Yellow-Bellied Sea Snake

Zz
Zebra Spitting Cobra